HOMEWORK ON YOUR COMPUTER

Asha Kalbag & Jonathan Sheikh-Miller

Designed and illustrated by Russell Punter
Edited by Philippa Wingate

Technical consultants: Derek Huby and Lisa Hughes
Additional consultancy by Cathy Wickens

Managing designer: Stephen Wright
Cover by Isaac Quaye
With thanks to Nicola Butler

Homework on your computer

Contents

Why do homework on a computer?

Computers are great for doing homework. When you do a piece of work on a computer, you can correct your mistakes without it showing. You can also experiment with different ways of presenting your work without having to copy the information out again and again.

Computers are also useful for gathering information to use in your homework. This is known as research. Computers even let you contact students and teachers across the world to get help with problems and exchange ideas.

Once you get used to doing homework on your computer, you will find you can produce impressive-looking work quickly and easily.

About this book

Homework on your Computer shows you how to use a computer to find information, and present it effectively using words and pictures. It also explains how to store and print any computer documents you create.

In this book, there are examples of the sorts of homework you can do on your computer. The examples are shown with numbered instructions and pictures, like the ones below. Each number on a picture indicates what you will see on your computer screen when you follow the matching instruction.

This example demonstrates how to draw a flag.

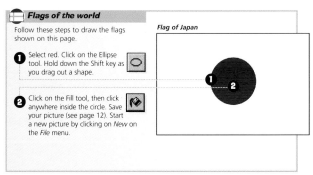

Flags of the world

Follow these steps to draw the flags shown on this page.

1 Select red. Click on the Ellipse tool. Hold down the Shift key as you drag out a shape.

2 Click on the Fill tool, then click anywhere inside the circle. Save your picture (see page 12). Start a new picture by clicking on *New* on the *File* menu.

Flag of Japan

The first instruction explains how to draw a circle. The second instruction explains how to make it red.

Using the Internet

The Internet, or "Net", is a network of computers all over the world that have been joined together so they can share information. Pages 28 to 41 of this book show you how the Internet can help you with your homework.

To take advantage of all the Internet has to offer, you need to use a computer that is connected to it. You can find advice on connecting your home computer to the Internet on page 43.

These pictures show you some of the ways you can use your computer to do homework.

You can look up information stored on the Internet. Find out how on pages 28 to 41.

 ## What do you need?

To follow the instructions in this book you need a computer that has Microsoft® Windows® 95 or 98. All the programs used for the examples in this book are included with these versions of Microsoft Windows. You can find out how to start programs in Microsoft Windows 95 and 98 on page 45.

On page 44 you can find out exactly what computer equipment you need for the activities in this book.

You can change the style of the words in your homework. See how on pages 6 and 7.

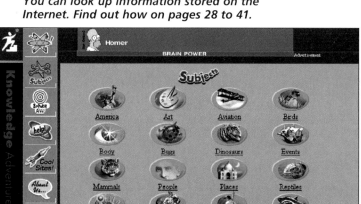

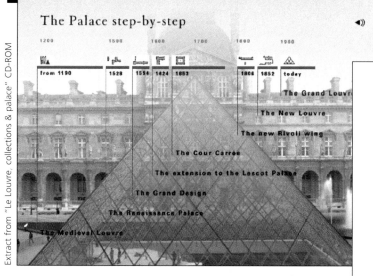

You can find facts and figures on "reference CD-ROMs". Find out more on pages 22 to 27.

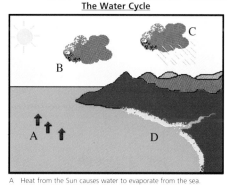

See pages 18 and 19 for advice on adding pictures to your homework.

The Water Cycle

A Heat from the Sun causes water to evaporate from the sea.
B Moist air rises, and clouds are formed.
C Winds carry clouds over land. Rain falls.
D Rivers carry water back to the sea, and the cycle continues.

You can create diagrams to illustrate your homework. Pages 14 to 17 show you how.

Word processing

Computers make it easy for you to type up your homework, correct it, and lay it out attractively. This is known as word processing. To do it, you need a word processing program.

WordPad

This book shows a program called WordPad, which comes with Microsoft Windows. Other word processing programs work in a similar way.

You can find out how to open WordPad on page 45. Computer programs appear on screen in rectangles called windows. The main part of WordPad's window is a blank area, called a page. This is where you type in your words. Above the page are some buttons and other controls. You will use these to tell WordPad to do different things with the words you type.

Type in your work. If you need help using your keyboard, turn to page 46. As you type, WordPad will line up the words with the left side of the page. You can rearrange them later following the instructions on page 5. On pages 5 and 46, you can find out how to correct any mistakes you make as you type.

abc Selecting words

Once you have typed up your work, you can rearrange the words or change their appearance. To do this, you first need to indicate the words you want to alter. This process is called selecting.

To select some words, move your mouse pointer to the left of them, and press down your left mouse button. Keeping the button pressed down, drag your mouse across the words. The words which your mouse pointer passes over will be highlighted. Release your mouse button when your chosen words are highlighted.

To "deselect" the words, simply click on another part of the page area.

In this example, part of the title of the poem shown on page 5 has been selected.

First night of the play

This is a WordPad window.

This row of buttons is called the tool bar.

This is called the menu bar.

Find out about these controls on page 6.

This flashing line is called a cursor. It indicates where the words you type will appear.

This row of controls is called the format bar.

Find out about this button on page 8.

Discover what these buttons do on page 7.

Learn about these buttons on page 5.

This is the page area.

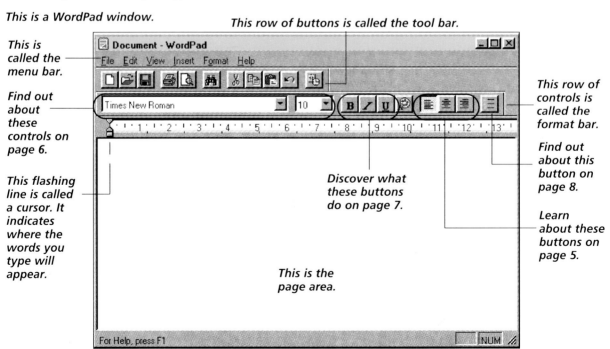

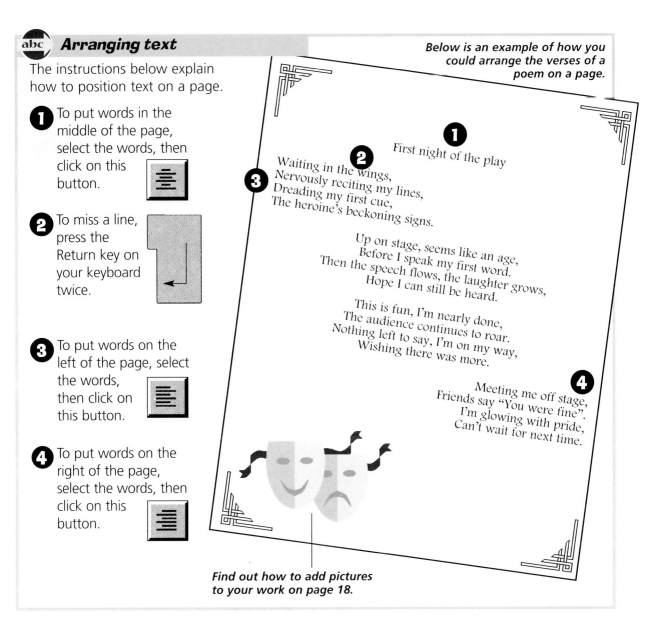 Arranging text

The instructions below explain how to position text on a page.

1 To put words in the middle of the page, select the words, then click on this button.

2 To miss a line, press the Return key on your keyboard twice.

3 To put words on the left of the page, select the words, then click on this button.

4 To put words on the right of the page, select the words, then click on this button.

Below is an example of how you could arrange the verses of a poem on a page.

1 First night of the play

2
Waiting in the wings,
Nervously reciting my lines,
Dreading my first cue,
The heroine's beckoning signs.

3
Up on stage, seems like an age,
Before I speak my first word.
Then the speech flows, the laughter grows,
Hope I can still be heard.

This is fun, I'm nearly done,
The audience continues to roar.
Nothing left to say, I'm on my way,
Wishing there was more.

4
Meeting me off stage,
Friends say "You were fine".
I'm glowing with pride,
Can't wait for next time.

Find out how to add pictures to your work on page 18.

Removing text

With a word processing program, you can easily remove or "delete" letters, words or whole sentences. This is useful if you make a mistake when you are typing, or if you change your mind about the content of your work.

To delete a word or sentence, select the text, then press the Delete key on your keyboard. If you delete some text by mistake, don't panic. Click on the Undo button on WordPad's tool bar and the text will reappear.

The Undo button

Finishing off

Each time you use a computer program to do some homework, you should store or "save" your work before you close the program. You can find out how to do this on pages 12 and 13. Once you have saved your work, you can close the program and turn off your computer. When you turn on your computer again, your work will still be there for you to look at, make changes to, or print. If you don't save your work, you will lose it when you close the program or turn off the computer.

Letter styles

When you use a computer, you can choose from different styles of letters and numbers, known as fonts. By using different fonts, you can make your homework look more exciting. You can also use a variety of methods to make some words stand out from the others on the page.

Fonts

WordPad automatically uses a font called Times New Roman, unless you change it. You can tell which font and size of letters WordPad is using by looking at two boxes on the format bar.

This is part of WordPad's format bar.

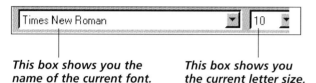

This box shows you the name of the current font.

This box shows you the current letter size.

Boxes like these, with small arrows on the right, are called drop-down list boxes. You can use these two to change the font and letter size of a piece of text (see page 7).

Choosing from lists

To use a drop-down list box, click on its arrow. A list of choices will drop down. To choose a new one, simply click on it.

An example drop-down list

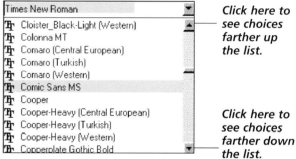

Click here to see choices farther up the list.

Click here to see choices farther down the list.

These examples show you some different fonts and give you advice on when to include them in your homework.

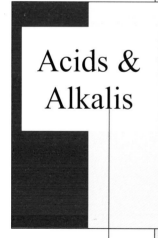

Times New Roman is good for typing pieces of work such as reports or results of science experiments because it is easy to read.

Courier gives the impression that a document was produced on an old typewriter.

Stencil makes it look like you have used an old-fashioned stamp.

Use Playbill on posters to make it look as though they were printed in the 19th century.

abC *Changing text appearance*

This section shows you how to change the appearance of text.

To change the font of a piece of text, first select the text. On the format bar, click on the arrow in the font drop-down list box. An alphabetical list of names of fonts will appear. Click on one.

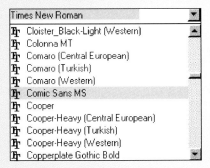

To change the size of the letters in a word, first select them. On the format bar, click on the arrow in the letter size drop-down list box. Choose another size from the list. The best sizes for long sections of text are sizes 10 and 12. Use bigger sizes, such as sizes 18 or 24, for headings.

Here are some actual letter sizes:

size 10   size 12

size 18 size 24

 To make words *italic*, select them, then click on this button on the format bar.

 To make words **bold**, select them, then click on this button on the format bar.

 To <u>underline</u> words, select them, then click on this button on the format bar.

This poster shows you some ways of emphasizing pieces of text.

❶ TRAVEL ON THE *TITANIC*, THE QUEEN OF THE OCEAN

❷ Take part in history and be one of the first to travel on the *Titanic*, White Star Line's luxury liner, for her maiden voyage from Southampton to New York.

❸ The *Titanic* is the largest man-made moving object in the world, but she is **unsinkable**. ❹ She has been designed with the safety and comfort of her passengers in mind. No expense has been spared. There is a swimming pool, gymnasium and Turkish bath on board, and the first and second class rooms are lavishly decorated.

The *Titanic* leaves Southampton at noon on April 10, 1912.

❺ <u>TICKETS ON SALE HERE</u>

Be careful not to use too many different fonts and sizes, as your work could look untidy and confusing.

This font is called Copperplate Gothic .

7

Organizing information

Some pieces of information, such as numbers, or words and their meanings, are easier to understand and interpret when they are organized into lists or tables.

Livening up lists

When each item in a list is of equal importance, such as recipe ingredients or different types of joints, you can put a small black dot, called a bullet, in front of each one.

1 In WordPad, type out your list, starting a new line for each item by pressing the Return key (see page 46). When you have finished, select the whole list. Click on the Bullets button on the format bar. Deselect the list by clicking on a blank part of the page.

2 Press the Return key. Click on the Bullets button again. This will stop WordPad adding bullets to the words you type next.

This piece of work includes information which is presented in a list.

The human skeleton

The human skeleton supports the body and protects vital organs such as the brain, lungs and heart. It is made of bone and cartilage. Cartilage is found in between bones. It is softer than bone and acts as a shock absorber, cushioning bones during movement.

Joints

A joint is where two or more bones meet. There are four main types of joints in the **1** human body. They are:

- Fixed joints such as those in the skull
- Sliding joints such as the wrist and ankle
- Hinge joints such as the elbow and knee
- Ball and socket joints such as the hip and shoulder **2**

Ask your teacher

Schoolwork can look very impressive when it is produced on a computer. But don't forget that the content of your work is more important than its appearance. You won't get good grades for incorrect or badly researched work, no matter how great it looks.

Sometimes teachers want particular pieces of homework to be written out by hand. If you are thinking of word processing a piece of work, it is a good idea to check with your teacher that this is acceptable.

Moving text

If you want to move a word, sentence or paragraph farther up or down the page, you don't have to delete it and type it out again. Instead, you can move it using a technique called dragging and dropping.

Select the word or phrase, then click on the selected area and hold down your left mouse button. Drag your mouse pointer to a new position, then release the button. You can only drag and drop a piece of text within the part of the page that already contains text.

Simple tables

You can use WordPad to put information, such as the results of a science experiment, in a table formed from columns.

1 Decide how far from the left side of the page you want each column heading to start. For example, the first column heading could start 4cm (1½in.) from the left and the second one could start 8cm (3in.) from the left. Click on the ruler above the page area at 4cm (1½in.) and at 8cm (3in.). Small black marks called tab stops will appear on the ruler.

This is part of a WordPad window.

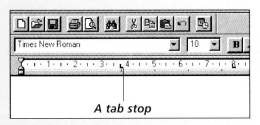

A tab stop

This example shows the results of a science experiment arranged into a table.

See page 7 to find out how to make headings bold.

Find out how to include pictures in your work on page 18.

You can create tables with more than two columns by creating more than two tab stops.

2 To enter a heading in the first column, press the Tab key on your keyboard. Type the heading. To enter a heading in the second column, press the Tab key again, and type the second heading.

3 Decide how far from the left you want each column of information to start. For example, the first one could start at 5cm (2in.) and the second one could start at 10.5cm (4in.). Press the Return key, then move the tab stops by clicking on them and dragging them along the ruler. To remove a tab stop completely, drag it to the far left of the ruler.

4 To put numbers (or text) in the columns, press the Tab key, then type the first number of the first column. Press the Tab key again before you type the first number of the second column. Press the Return key to start a new line. Repeat this process for each line of numbers.

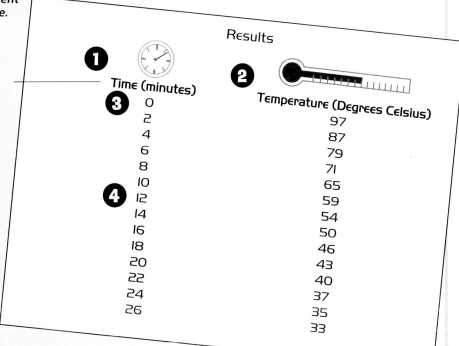

Results

Time (minutes)	Temperature (Degrees Celsius)
0	97
2	87
4	79
6	71
8	65
10	59
12	54
14	50
16	46
18	43
20	40
22	37
24	35
26	33

Organizing your work

This section shows you how to create a specific place on your computer where you can keep all the homework you do.

 ## Files and folders

Your computer stores every piece of work you decide to keep as a collection of data known as a file. Computer files can be put inside folders, just as you might organize pieces of paper into a cardboard folder.

Your computer stores files and folders on devices called disks. The main disk you will use is inside your computer. This is called the hard disk. You can use a program called Windows Explorer to see what files and folders are already stored on your computer's hard disk.

When you open Windows Explorer (see page 45) you will see a window like the one below. It contains small pictures called icons. These represent different disks, folders and files.

 ## Exploring your computer

Windows Explorer's window is divided into two parts or "panes": a left pane and a right pane. When you click on a disk or folder icon in the left pane, icons representing the contents of this disk or folder will appear in the right pane.

 ## A homework folder

As well as showing you what files and folders are stored on your computer, Windows Explorer also lets you create new folders for storing files. You could make a folder called "Homework" for storing your homework files. You could also create different subject folders within your Homework folder. Find out how on page 11.

This is a Windows Explorer window.

The icons in the right pane may be arranged in rows, as shown here, or in a list, as shown on page 11.

Menu bar —
Tool bar —

This icon represents the hard disk.

This is the left pane.

A folder icon

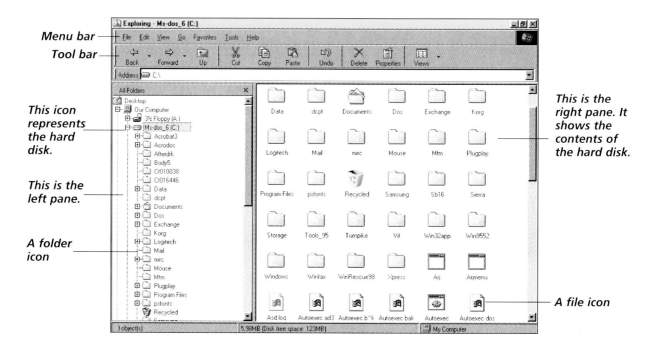

This is the right pane. It shows the contents of the hard disk.

A file icon

Creating folders

Here are instructions for creating new folders on your computer:

These screen shots show the different stages of creating new folders on your computer.

1 Open Windows Explorer, following the instructions on page 45. Click on the icon for your computer's hard disk in the left pane of the window. This is usually the one with (C:) in its name.

2 Click on *File* on the menu bar. A list, or "menu", will appear. Point to *New*. A submenu will appear. Click on *Folder*.

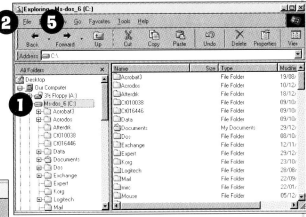

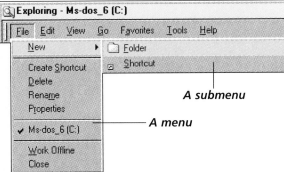

A submenu

A menu

3 An icon with the temporary name New Folder will appear at the bottom of the right pane. Type the word Homework, then press the Return key.

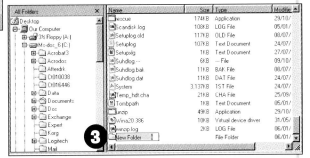

4 An icon for your Homework folder will appear in the left pane. Double-click on this icon.

5 Point to *New* on the *File* menu again. Click on *Folder*.

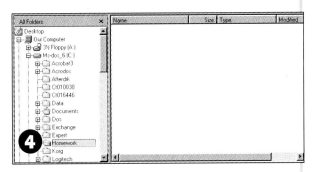

6 Another New Folder icon will appear in the right pane. Type the name of a subject you are studying, for example, Geography, then press the Return key.

Repeat steps 4, 5 and 6 to create a folder for each of the subjects you are studying.

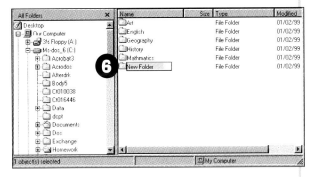

Saving your work

Y ou should store or "save" all your homework in your Homework folder (see page 11). Once you have saved a file, you can close it without losing any of the information it contains. You can also open it later to make changes to it, or print it out (see page 20).

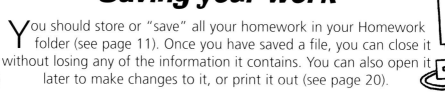

Saving files

These steps show how to save some work that is on screen into your Homework folder. It is a good idea to do this as you begin your work.

Below you can see what will appear on your screen as you work through the instructions.

1 Click on *File* on the menu bar. A menu will appear.

2 Click on *Save As...* A box called a dialog box will appear. You use dialog boxes to give information to your computer.

A dialog box

3 Click on the arrow in the drop-down list box called Save in to open a list of parts of your computer.

4 Click on the icon for your computer's hard drive. Icons for the folders on the hard drive will appear in the main part of the dialog box.

5 Click on the icon for your Homework folder. Then click on the Open button.

Open button

6 Click on the icon for the relevant subject folder. For example, to save a piece of science homework, click on the Science icon. Click on the Open button again.

7 Select the text in the box called File name. Type a descriptive name for your file, so you can remember which piece of homework it contains, for example, **photosynthesis**. Your computer will not let you use any of these symbols in the filename: **/*<>?":|**.

8 Finally, click on the Save button.

Saving changes

If you make more changes to a file that you have already saved, you don't have to follow the steps on page 12 to save the changes. Instead, you can save them by opening the *File* menu and clicking on *Save*. Some programs, including WordPad, also have a Save button that you can click on.

WordPad's Save button

Opening an existing file

Follow the steps below to open a file you have saved previously.

1 Open the program you used to create the file, for example WordPad. Click on *File* on the menu bar. A menu will appear.

2 Click on *Open...* A dialog box will appear.

3 Click on the arrow in the drop-down list box called Look in.

4 A list of parts of your computer will drop down. Click on the icon for your computer's hard drive. Icons for the folders that are on the hard drive will appear in the main part of the dialog box.

5 Click on the icon for your Homework folder. Then click on the Open button.

6 Click on the icon for the subject folder where you saved the file. Then click on the Open button again. You will see a list of names of some of the files that you have previously saved in that folder.

7 Click on the name of the file you want to open. If the file you are looking for isn't listed, click on the arrow in the drop-down list box called Files of type. Select All Documents or All Files from the list. Your computer will list all the files that the folder contains.

8 Finally, click on the Open button.

Below you can see what will appear on your screen as you work through the instructions.

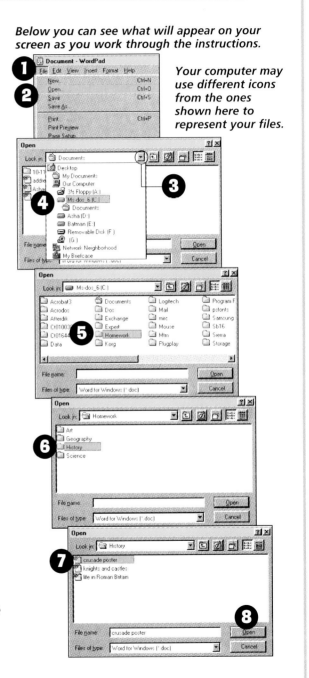

Your computer may use different icons from the ones shown here to represent your files.

13

Computer pictures

Save time and get great results by using your computer to create pictures for your homework. With a couple of clicks of a mouse button, you can neatly draw shapes such as squares and circles, and fill them in evenly.

Painting programs

The simplest type of program for creating pictures on a computer is a painting program. Microsoft Windows includes one called Paint. You can find out how to open Paint on page 45.

Paint's window is shown on the right. In the middle, there is an area where you paint your pictures. It may help to think of this area as an on-screen canvas.

On the left of the canvas, there is a collection of buttons called the tool box. These buttons represent painting and drawing tools. Hold your mouse over a button to see the name of the tool it represents.

At the bottom of the window, there is a paint box which contains different paints that you can use.

Tool box

This is a Paint window.

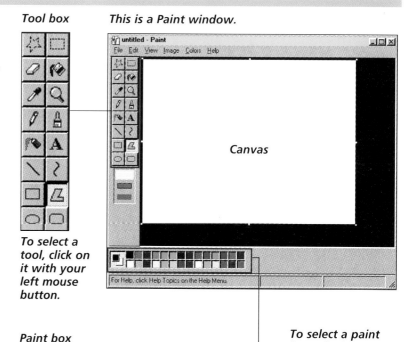

Canvas

To select a tool, click on it with your left mouse button.

Paint box

To select a paint from the box, click on a square with your left mouse button.

Picture size

You may want to add a picture you are about to draw to a WordPad document, or print it onto a particular size of paper. If so, you must make sure it will fit into the space available for it. Before you start painting, work out how high and wide you want the picture to be. You can then adjust the size of the canvas accordingly.

To do this, open the *Image* menu and click on *Attributes....* A dialog box called Attributes will open. Use the top part to change the size of the canvas. For example, each of the flags on page 15 is drawn on a canvas 9.2cm (3½in.) wide and 6cm (2¼in.) high. To finish, click OK.

This is the top part of the Attributes dialog box.

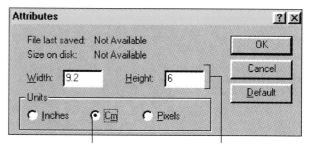

Click with your mouse in one of these circles to choose a unit of measurement.

To change the dimensions of the canvas, type new numbers here.

Flags of the world

You can draw the flags shown on this page by following these steps.

Flag of Japan

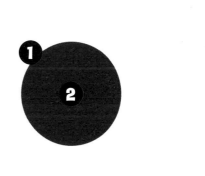

 Select red. Click on the Ellipse tool. Hold down the Shift key as you drag out a shape.

 Click on the Fill tool, then click anywhere inside the circle. Save your picture (see page 12). Start a new picture by clicking on *New* on the *File* menu.

Flag of Italy

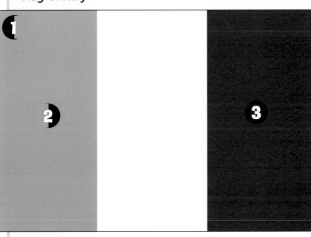

1 Select green. Click on the Rectangle tool and drag out a rectangle shape.

2 Click on the Fill tool, then click anywhere inside the rectangle.

3 Repeat steps 1 and 2 using red paint. Save your picture. Click on *New* on the *File* menu to start a new picture.

You can use the Rectangle tool to add a border.

 Select dark blue. Click on the rectangle tool. Draw a rectangle.

 Click on the Fill tool, then click anywhere inside the rectangle.

 Click on the Polygon tool. Draw a line. Release your mouse button to change direction. Join the last line to the first line to close the star.

 Click on the Fill tool, then click anywhere inside the star.

 Repeat steps 1 to 4 with red paint. Save your picture.

Flag of Panama

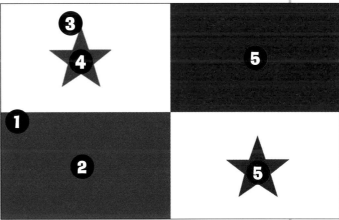

Drawing diagrams

nce you have had some painting practice, you can use Paint to create more complex pictures and diagrams. For example, you could draw a diagram for your geography or science homework.

Tool options

Some painting tools can produce more than one effect. For example, the Line tool can draw lines of different thicknesses. When you click on a tool, the different effects it can produce will appear at the bottom of the tool box. Click on the one you want before you use the tool.

You can specify the thickness of the lines that a shape tool, such as the Rectangle tool, will use to draw shapes. To do this, first click on the Line tool, then click on the width of line you want. Next click on a shape tool and draw a shape. Its outline will be as thick as the line you chose.

The Line tool

The options for the Line tool

Useful tools

Two tools which are useful for drawing complicated pictures are the Magnifier tool and the Eraser tool.

The Magnifier tool enables you to see, and work on, a close-up of part of your picture. To use it, click on the Magnifier tool button, then click on the part of the picture that you want to magnify. A close-up of that part of the picture will appear. To see your picture at normal size again, click on the Magnifier tool button again, then click anywhere on your picture.

The Magnifier tool

You use the Eraser tool to cover up mistakes. Click on the Eraser tool button, then drag your mouse over the mistake. The Eraser tool will cover the mistake with white paint. You can make the Eraser tool use another type of paint. To do this, click on your chosen paint with your right mouse button before you use the tool.

The Eraser tool

Water cycle diagram

Follow these instructions to draw a diagram of the water cycle like the one shown on page 17.

1 Use the Attributes dialog box to make the canvas 8cm (3in.) wide and 5cm (2in.) high.

2 Click on the Line tool. Choose the third width option. Click on the Rectangle tool and draw a frame around the edge of the canvas.

3 Click on the Pencil tool and draw the outline of the land. Make sure the lines join up with the frame.

4 Click on the Line tool and choose the narrowest width. Draw the horizon.

5 Select a pale blue and click on the Fill tool. Click anywhere above the horizon. Select a darker blue. Click anywhere below the horizon.

6 Use the Fill tool to paint the land. Use green or brown paint for the nearest land and dull shades for the distant hills.

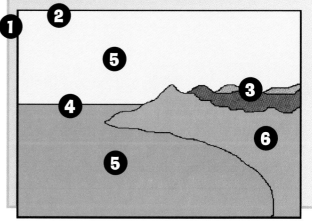

An illustration of the water cycle

You could use the Line tool to add rays of sunshine.

This text is a WordPad document. Find out how to insert your pictures into text documents on page 18.

You could use the Airbrush tool to add shading to the clouds.

The Water Cycle

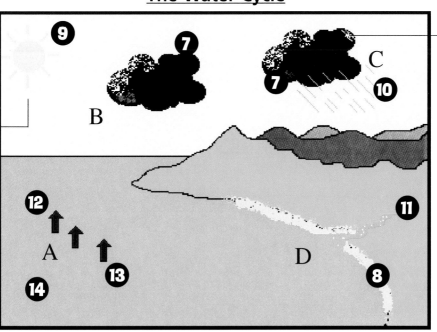

A   Heat from the Sun causes water to evaporate from the sea.
B   Moist air rises, and clouds are formed.
C   Winds carry clouds over land. Rain falls.
D   Rivers carry water back to the sea, and the cycle continues.

7 Select black and click on the Ellipse tool. Draw an oval. Click on the Fill tool and paint the inside of the oval. Draw and fill a few overlapping ovals to form a cloud shape. Draw two clouds.

8 Select yellow and click on the Airbrush tool. Draw the beach.

9 Click on the Ellipse tool. Hold down the Shift key and draw a circle. Use the Fill tool to fill in the Sun.

10 Select dark blue and click on the Line tool. Hold down the Shift key to draw the rain.

11 Select dark blue and click on the Brush tool. Draw the river. Use a thicker stroke for the part near the sea.

12 Select black and click on the Line tool. Hold the Shift key down and draw an arrow. Use the Fill tool to make it red.

13 Click on the Select tool and drag it diagonally across the arrow. A box will appear around the arrow. Hold down the Control key and drag the box to duplicate the arrow. Repeat this process.

14 Select black and click on the Text tool. Drag it diagonally to draw a box. Type a letter. If necessary, select *Text Toolbar* from the *View* menu. Use the dialog box that appears to change the font or letter size (see page 7). Click outside the text box to finish. Finally, save your picture (see page 12).

Working with pictures

Once you have created a picture on your computer, you can use it to illustrate a piece of work that you have word processed. You can also buy pictures drawn by other people that you can use to illustrate your homework. These pictures are known as clip art.

Copying and pasting

The easiest way to include a picture in a text document is by using a method called copying and pasting. These instructions explain how to copy a picture drawn in Paint, and add it to a report written in WordPad.

1 Start Paint and open the file containing the picture that you want to copy.

2 Open the *Edit* menu and click on *Select All*. A line will appear around the picture.

3 Open the *Edit* menu and click on *Copy*.

4 Start WordPad, then open the file containing the report in which you want to include the picture.

5 Position the cursor at the point in your text where you want the picture to appear.

6 Open WordPad's *Edit* menu and click on *Paste*. The picture will appear where the cursor was. It will be surrounded by a frame with eight squares, known as handles.

7 Click anywhere off the picture. The frame will disappear. Save your document.

Any text which comes after the picture will be pushed down onto another line.

These pictures show you what you will see if you copy a diagram about global warming and paste it into a text document.

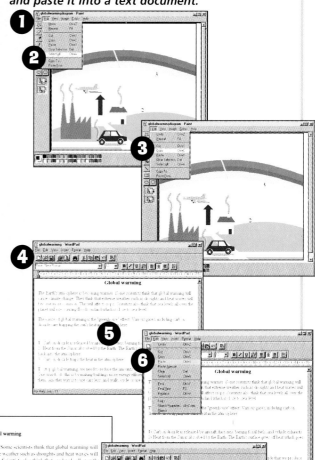

Repositioning a picture

Once you have added a picture to a WordPad document, you can move it around the text area by dragging and dropping it. To do this, place your mouse pointer over the picture, then press down the left mouse button. Drag your mouse pointer to a new position, then release the mouse button. The picture will move to the new location.

You can also position a picture in the middle, left or right of the page. Select the picture by clicking on it, then click on one of the position buttons on the format bar (see page 5).

Resizing a picture

To make a picture you have inserted into a WordPad document bigger or smaller, click on the picture. A frame with eight handles will appear. When you position your mouse over a handle, it changes into one of the shapes shown on the left. You can resize the picture by clicking on a handle and dragging it.

You will find pictures similar to these in a clip art collection.

Changing a picture

To make changes to a picture in a WordPad document, double-click on it. A Paint window containing the picture will open. There will be a frame around the picture. Make the changes you want, then click outside the frame. Any changes you have made will be shown on the picture in the WordPad document.

You can only use this method to make changes to pictures that you have drawn yourself. You can't use it to alter other pictures, such as clip art (see below).

This is what you will see when you double-click on a picture in WordPad.

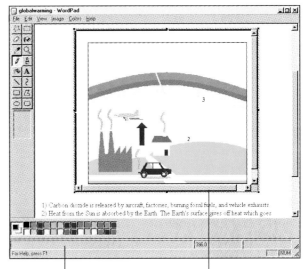

Paint window   Frame

Clip art pictures

Clip art pictures are ready-made pictures that you can include in your computer documents. Clip art is sometimes included with computer programs. You can also buy it from places that sell computer equipment and software. It comes in collections of thousands of drawings or photographs stored on CD-ROMs. There are many different collections available.

Only include clip art pictures in your homework if they are relevant. Don't use them just to fill up space.

Printing your work

This section shows you how to print your homework onto paper. As a part of the printing process, you will need to instruct your computer how to arrange your work on a piece of paper.

▨ *Printing*

These instructions are for printing out a piece of work produced in WordPad or Paint. Before you start, make sure your printer is switched on and that it contains paper.

1 Start the program you used to create the piece of work you want to print. Open up the document or picture so that it is displayed on screen (see page 13).

2 Click on *Page Setup...* on the *File* menu. A Page Setup dialog box will appear.

3 Choose the same paper size as the paper in your printer. If you want, change the printing orientation and the sizes of the margins (see below). Any changes you make will affect the arrangement of the words or picture on the page.

4 Click on Printer. Another part of the dialog box will open. Choose the name of the printer you are using from the drop-down list. Click OK. Then, click OK again to close the Page Setup dialog box.

These screen shots show you what you will see as you prepare your document for printing.

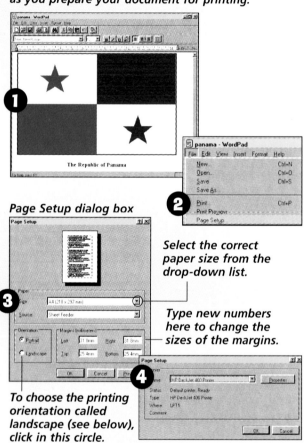

Page Setup dialog box

Select the correct paper size from the drop-down list.

Type new numbers here to change the sizes of the margins.

To choose the printing orientation called landscape (see below), click in this circle.

▢ *Printing orientation*

Printers can print words and pictures onto paper in two ways, known as printing orientations. The two orientations are called portrait and landscape. Portrait is when the short side of the paper is at the top. Landscape is when the long side of the paper is at the top. Use portrait orientation for most documents, including letters and reports. Use landscape orientation for posters and pictures only.

Portrait

Bats
Bats are the only mammals that can fly. There are over 900 different species of bats. They can be divided into two groups: insect-eating bats and fruit bats.
All bats are nocturnal. This means they are awake at night. They spend the day sleeping in caves, treetops or old buildings.

Insect-eating bats
Insect-eating bats eat moths, gnats and mosquitoes. They usually live near rivers or lakes where there are lots of insects. They find the insects using a process called echo-location. This

Landscape

WINTERBOURNE HIGH SCHOOL DRAMATIC SOCIETY
presents
A Midsummer Night's Dream
by William Shakespeare
Wed 28 - Sat 31 July
The New School Hall, Winterbourne High School
Tickets available from school office

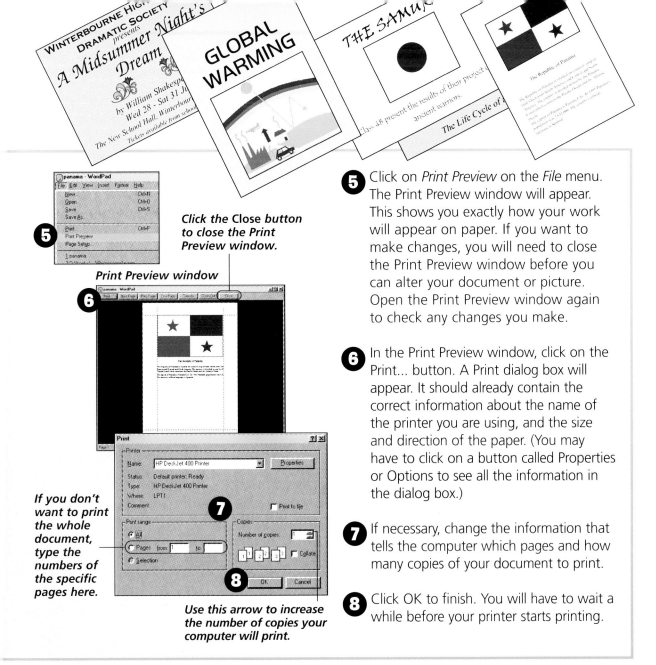

Click the Close button to close the Print Preview window.

Print Preview window

If you don't want to print the whole document, type the numbers of the specific pages here.

Use this arrow to increase the number of copies your computer will print.

5 Click on *Print Preview* on the *File* menu. The Print Preview window will appear. This shows you exactly how your work will appear on paper. If you want to make changes, you will need to close the Print Preview window before you can alter your document or picture. Open the Print Preview window again to check any changes you make.

6 In the Print Preview window, click on the Print... button. A Print dialog box will appear. It should already contain the correct information about the name of the printer you are using, and the size and direction of the paper. (You may have to click on a button called Properties or Options to see all the information in the dialog box.)

7 If necessary, change the information that tells the computer which pages and how many copies of your document to print.

8 Click OK to finish. You will have to wait a while before your printer starts printing.

Margins

A margin is a blank area between the edge of your work and the edge of the paper. Each page of work you print will have four margins: left, right, top and bottom. Each one can be a different width.

Your computer will automatically choose a width for each margin, but you can change these. If you are printing a page of words, such as a letter or report, make sure all four margins are at least 15mm (½ in.) wide. The left and right margins should be the same width as each other. When you change the width of the margins, your computer will automatically rearrange the words on the page.

You can experiment with different margin widths when you print out other types of homework, such as posters, pictures or covers for your projects.

CD-ROM basics

One way you can use your computer to research your homework is by looking up information on a reference CD-ROM. These usually contain information in the form of pictures, words and sounds, and sometimes animations or short video clips.

Obtaining CD-ROMs

There are reference CD-ROMs available on many different subjects. You may have been given one or two with your computer. If not, you can buy reference CD-ROMs from places that sell computer software. Some of them are quite expensive, so find out first whether you can borrow them from your school or library. Also, look out for computer magazines that include free reference CD-ROMs.

Before you buy or borrow a CD-ROM, read the information on the box to make sure you can use it on the type of computer you have. You can find out what basic equipment you need to use CD-ROMs on page 44.

This screen shot is from a CD-ROM about the human body called BodyWorks 5.0.

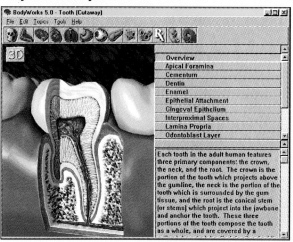

Using a CD-ROM

To use a CD-ROM that you have already installed (see the box below), insert the disc into your computer's CD-ROM drive and close the drive. Some CD-ROMs start automatically. You need to start others yourself. You will find instructions for starting CD-ROMs on page 45.

One of the first things you will see is a screen which is a starting point for exploring the information on the CD-ROM. Before this screen appears, you may see some information about the company that made the CD-ROM.

This screen is the starting point for exploring a CD-ROM called the Usborne Animated Children's Encyclopedia.

To explore the CD-ROM, you need to open the chest by clicking on the key and dragging it to the keyhole.

Installing a CD-ROM

Before you can use any CD-ROM, you will need to copy some computer files from the CD-ROM onto your computer's hard disk. This process is known as installing. The files that you copy will enable your computer to display the information which is stored on the CD-ROM. You only have to install a CD-ROM the first time you use it. You will find instructions for installing a CD-ROM in the booklet that comes with it.

CD-ROM encyclopedias

A useful reference CD-ROM for homework research is a CD-ROM encyclopedia. Like a printed encyclopedia, it contains facts about all kinds of different subjects.

The projects on pages 24 and 25 use two CD-ROM encyclopedias, the *Usborne Animated* *Children's Encyclopedia* and *Microsoft® Encarta® Encyclopedia,* to demonstrate how to find and use information on a CD-ROM.

Don't worry if you don't have these particular CD-ROMs. You will find that most CD-ROMs work in the same way.

Links

As you explore CD-ROMs, you'll come across words and pictures which do particular things when you click on them. For example, they may display the definition of a word, show you an animation, or play a piece of music. These words and pictures are known as hotspots or hyperlinks.

There are a few ways of identifying a hyperlink. Sometimes the words are underlined or highlighted. Often your mouse pointer will change shape when you rest it over a hyperlink. It usually changes into a hand shape like the one shown here:

This picture shows the different types of hyperlinks included in the Usborne Animated Children's Encyclopedia.

If you click on an icon of a TV set, you will see an animation.

If you click on a gold star in a picture, you will see more information about the picture.

If you click on an icon showing a loudspeaker, you will hear the text next to it being read aloud.

If you click on a highlighted or underlined word, you will see its definition.

If you click on an arrow, another screen of facts on the same topic will appear.

CD-ROM research

A CD-ROM can contain masses of information. For example, all the information in a 32 volume encyclopedia can fit onto a single compact disc. It's important to understand the different techniques for locating information on a CD-ROM.

science **Finding information by category**

On many CD-ROMs, the information is organized into subject categories. There will be a screen that shows these categories. You find information by looking in the relevant one. This example shows how to find information about the skeleton on the *Usborne Animated Children's Encyclopedia.*

These pictures show the screens you will see as you look for information about the human skeleton.

Key

Keyhole

1 From the starting screen, open the chest by clicking on the key, then dragging it to the keyhole. The next screen shows several scrolls tied with ribbons which represent the categories, for example Science, People and Nature.

Science category

Rest your mouse over a picture on a scroll to see the name of the category.

2 Click on the scroll called Science. A screen showing narrower subject categories will appear.

3 Click on the words The Human Body.

4 A screen showing information about the skeleton will appear.

These are the categories within the Science category.

A screen showing information about the human skeleton

These pictures are hyperlinks to other categories.

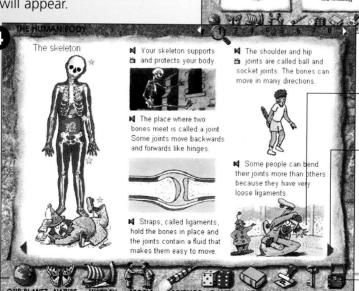

This picture moves when you rest your mouse pointer over it.

Click here for more information about the human body.

Click here to close the CD-ROM.

Word searches

Most CD-ROMs include a tool which will search for information containing a word or words of your choice. The instructions below explain how to use the search tool included with *Microsoft® Encarta® Encyclopedia* to locate entries or "articles" that contain the word **brain** in their titles. Search tools on other CD-ROMs work in a similar way.

1 Click on the words *Encyclopedia articles* on the starting screen. A dialog box called Pinpointer will appear.

2 Type the word **brain** in the blank strip at the top of the dialog box. The encyclopedia will list each entry that has this word in its title in the main part of the dialog box.

3 Click on the title of the article called Brain.

4 The dialog box will disappear and you will see information about the brain.

These pictures show the screens you will see as you look for entries with the word brain in their titles.

The Microsoft Encarta starting screen

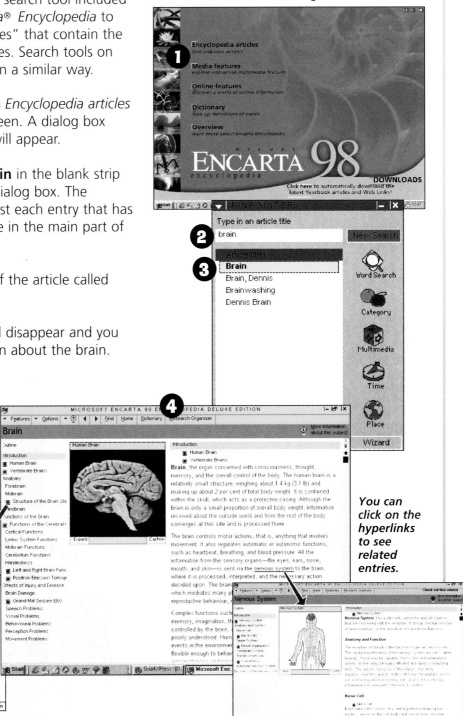

This picture shows the entry about the brain from the Microsoft Encarta Encyclopedia *CD-ROM.*

This is a list of other pictures or diagrams of the brain. Click on a name to see one.

You can click on the hyperlinks to see related entries.

Using information from a CD-ROM

When you find some useful information on a CD-ROM, you can print it out so that you can refer to it later on. Many CD-ROMs also let you copy text and pictures to include in your homework.

Printing from a CD-ROM

To print pictures and text that are displayed on your screen, look on screen for a button or menu item called *Print* (or something similar) and click on it.

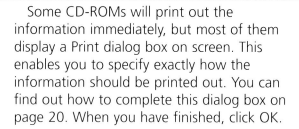

To print from the Usborne Animated Children's Encyclopedia, **click on this icon.**

Some CD-ROMs will print out the information immediately, but most of them display a Print dialog box on screen. This enables you to specify exactly how the information should be printed out. You can find out how to complete this dialog box on page 20. When you have finished, click OK.

Copying text

To copy text from a CD-ROM and paste it into a word processing program, such as WordPad, follow the steps below. (You may not be able to do this with some CD-ROMs.)

1 Display the text you want to copy on screen and select it with your mouse.

2 Look on screen for a button or menu item called *Copy*, *Copy Text*, *Copy Text Selection,* or something similar. Click on this. Your computer will copy the text that you selected.

3 Open WordPad. You will see a blank page. If you want to add the text to an existing document, open this (see page 13) and position the cursor where you want the text to appear.

4 Open the *Edit* menu and click on *Paste*.

5 The text you copied will appear in the WordPad document. The font and size of the letters will be the same as they are on the CD-ROM. Save your work (see page 12).

These pictures show what you will see as you copy text from a CD-ROM into a word processing program.

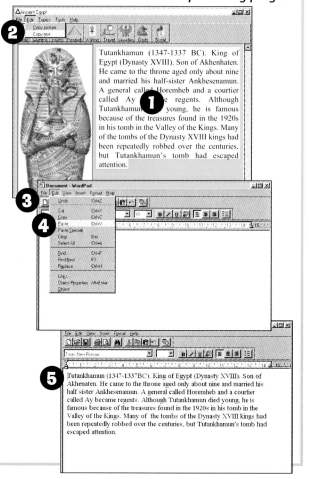

How can I use the information?

Most companies that make CD-ROMs don't mind if you use their pictures or text in a personal project as long as you include details of where you obtained the information. However, most companies forbid you to include the information in a document which will be distributed publicly, such as a school newspaper, without their permission. They will also object if you use the information to earn money.

CD-ROMs usually include a statement about how you can use the information they contain. Always check this before including text and pictures from a CD-ROM in your homework.

Use your own words

Don't copy large amounts of text from a CD-ROM into your homework. Instead, rewrite the information you find in your own words. Your teachers will want to read something you have written yourself, not something that other people have written.

It is OK to include a short extract of text from a CD-ROM to back up what you say in your homework. But, if you do this, make it clear that the words are not your own. You can separate the extract from your own text by putting it in italics (see page 7), or by enclosing it in quotation marks. Remember to include details of where the information comes from.

Copying pictures

These instructions explain how to copy pictures from a CD-ROM and paste them either into a painting program or a word processing program. (You may not be able to do this with some CD-ROMs.)

1 Display the picture you want to copy on screen.

2 Look on screen for a button or menu item called *Copy Image* (or something similar). Click on this.

3 Open WordPad or Paint. In WordPad you will see a blank page. In Paint you will see a blank canvas. If you want to add the picture to an existing WordPad document, open this (see page 13) and position the cursor where you want the picture to appear.

4 Go to the *Edit* menu and click on *Paste*.

5 The picture will appear in the Wordpad document or on the blank canvas in Paint. Save your work (see page 12).

These pictures show what you will see as you copy a picture from a CD-ROM into Paint.

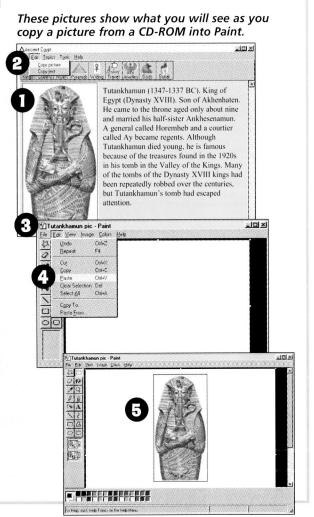

Introducing the Internet

The Internet or "Net" is a huge network of computers all over the world which are joined together so they can share information. It offers several different facilities. Two of these are particularly useful when doing homework – the World Wide Web or "Web", and electronic mail or "e-mail".

Electronic mail

E-mail is a method of sending messages from one computer to another. You can use a computer which is connected to the Internet to exchange messages with other Internet users. It doesn't matter which country they are in.

You can use e-mail to get specialist help with your homework, or discuss your studies with fellow students. It's also a great way to improve your skills in a foreign language. Find out more on pages 38 and 39.

The World Wide Web

The Web is a vast collection of information which is stored on the computers that make up the Internet. The information covers a wide range of subjects and is presented using words, pictures, sounds and video.

The Web is like an enormous library that you can use 24 hours a day, without leaving your computer. In addition, much of the information is regularly updated. This makes the Web a good source for the latest facts and figures.

The Web is made up of millions of computer documents called Web pages. A collection of Web pages which were put on the Web by one person or organization is called a Web site. All kinds of people and organizations put information on the Web.

You will come across Web pages similar to the ones shown below when you use the Web for research.

This Web page contains news from a Spanish newspaper called El Pais.

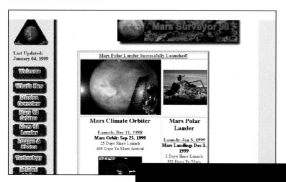

These pictures showing the surface of Mars were put on the Web by the United States National Aeronautics and Space Administration (NASA).

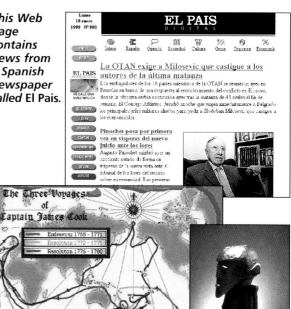

These exhibits are displayed on the Web site of the Hunterian Museum in Scotland.

Looking at Web pages

To look at Web pages, you need to use a program called a browser. A browser called Microsoft® Internet Explorer® is used for the examples in this book. Find out how to open it on page 45. There are other browsers available, but they all work in a similar way. If you have a different browser, you will still be able to follow the examples in this book.

   A browser copies information from the Web onto your computer, and displays it on your computer screen in a window like the one shown below. Copying information from the Web is known as downloading.

 ## Connecting to the Net

Before your browser can download Web pages, you need to connect your computer to the Internet, or "go on-line". Your computer may already be set up to go on-line. If it isn't, turn to page 43 to find out how to prepare your computer for using the Internet.

   When you open your browser, it may automatically instruct your computer to go online. If not, a message will appear asking if you want to connect to the Internet. Click OK or Yes. Once you are on-line, your browser will automatically download and display a Web page known as a start page.

Below you can see a Web page displayed by the Microsoft Internet Explorer browser.

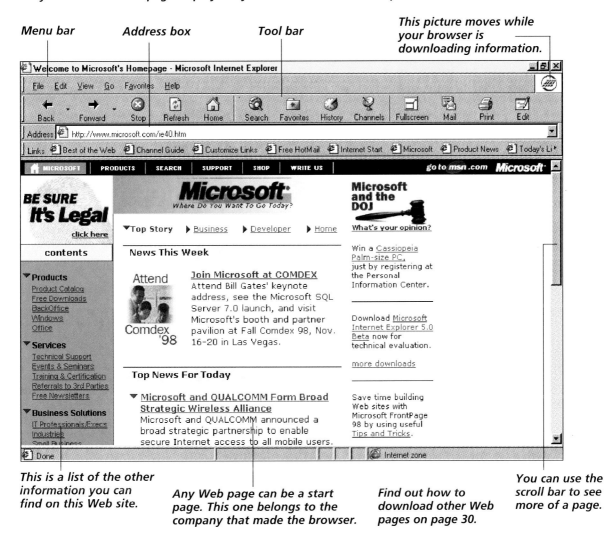

Menu bar   **Address box**   **Tool bar**   *This picture moves while your browser is downloading information.*

This is a list of the other information you can find on this Web site.

Any Web page can be a start page. This one belongs to the company that made the browser.

Find out how to download other Web pages on page 30.

You can use the scroll bar to see more of a page.

Exploring a Web site

This section shows you how to look for information on a Web site. Say, for example, you needed to find out about past presidents of the USA for your history homework. A good site to try is the White House Web site.

URL Downloading a particular page

The information on the Web is stored on many different computers. To make it easy to find Web pages, each one has a unique address called a Uniform Resource Locator (URL). The URL for the White House Web site's main or home page is **http://www.whitehouse.gov/**.

To download a Web page, type its URL carefully into your browser's Address box, then press the Return key. After a few seconds, the page should appear in your browser window. You will find out what to do when you don't know a Web page's address on page 32.

This picture shows the White House Web site's home page.

Web links

Web pages usually contain hyperlinks (see page 23). A hyperlink on a Web page will either link to another page on the same Web site, or to another Web site. When you click on a hyperlink, your browser will download and display another Web page.

These hyperlinks are from the White House Web site.

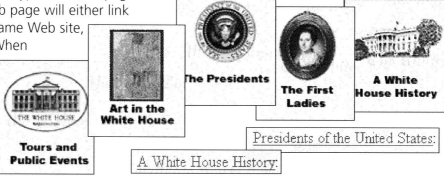

Using hyperlinks

The instructions below explain how to use the hyperlinks on the White House Web site to find information about past presidents. Other Web sites work in a similar way.

This is part of the White House Web site's home page.

1 Download the White House home page. Click on <u>White House History and Tours</u>.

2 On the next page, click on the picture of the presidential seal.

3 The next page contains a list of all the presidents of USA. Each name is a hyperlink. Click on one to see a page containing that president's biography.

4 Read about the president.

5 To return to the previous page, click on the Back button on your browser's tool bar.

6 Click on the name of another president to see a page of information about him.

The Presidents of the United States of America

You can tell that the names of the presidents are hyperlinks because they are underlined.

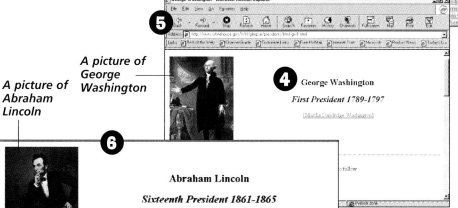

A picture of George Washington

A picture of Abraham Lincoln

4 George Washington
First President 1789-1797

[Martha Dandridge Washington]

6

Abraham Lincoln
Sixteenth President 1861-1865

[Mary Todd Lincoln]

Fun Fact: During the Civil War, telegraph wires were strung to follow the action on the battlefield. But there was no telegraph office in the White House, so Lincoln went across the street to the War Department to get the news.

The Web pages shown in this book may not look exactly the same when you download them. This is because people who maintain Web sites often update the information they contain or change the way it is organized or presented.

Searching the Web

Some Web pages contain programs called search engines which can help you find useful Web pages. Use them when you don't know where on the Web to find information on a particular subject. There are a number of different search engines but they all work in the same way.

Word searches

Search engines look for Web pages that contain words of your choice, known as key words. These could be the most important words from the title of your project. For example, if you have been told to find out about the exploration of space, you could choose **exploration** and **space**. You could also choose other words that are related to the subject, for example **rocket** or **satellite.**

Using a search engine

This section shows you how to use a search engine called AltaVista to search for pages about space exploration.

1 Go to AltaVista's home page at:
http://www.altavista.com/

2 Type your key word or words, for example, **space exploration**, into the empty box.

3 Click on the button called Search to instruct the program to look for Web pages that contain your key words.

4 Wait for the search engine to display a list containing descriptions of the pages it has found, and hyperlinks to them. This list may contain hundreds or thousands of hyperlinks. If so, it will be divided into several Web pages.

5 Click on a hyperlink that sounds useful to see a page about space exploration.

Address box

Part of AltaVista's home page

Type in words here.   **Click here to start a search.**

This page contains some of the results of AltaVista's search for space exploration.

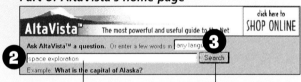
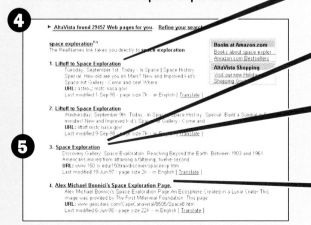

When you are looking for a particular piece of information, such as an account of the exploration of the moon, you won't want to look at hundreds of Web pages to find it. You can narrow down a key word search by giving a search engine more precise instructions about what to look for.

You can use as many key words as you like. To make sure a search engine only finds Web pages that contain them all, put a + sign in front of each word. For example, **+exploration +space +moon.** If you don't do this, the search engine will include pages that contain only one of the words when it produces a list of results.

To find Web pages where your key words appear next to each other, place quotation marks around them. This is useful when your key words are a name or phrase. For instance, to find Web pages about the astronaut Neil Armstrong, you would type **"Neil Armstrong"**.

Following the instructions above will help you to search efficiently with AltaVista and some other search engines. You will find a list of addresses for other search engines on page 42. However, some work in different ways. Always read a search engine's instructions to find out exactly how you can narrow down a search.

Below are some pages about space exploration found by AltaVista.

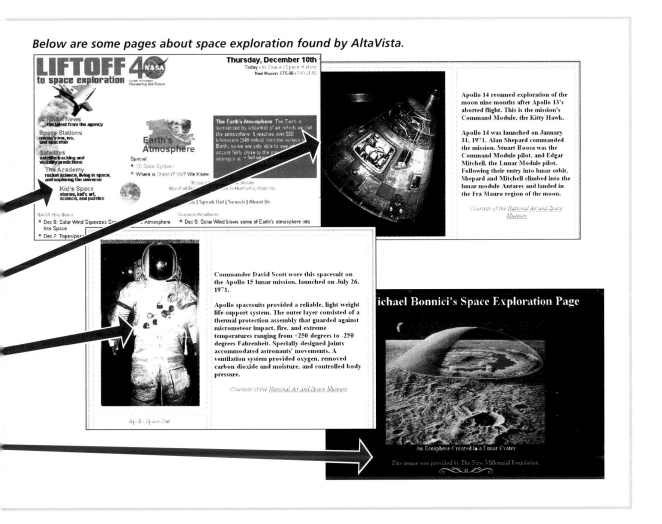

Using information from the Web

Once you have discovered some useful information on the Web, you can print it out, or copy it into a word processing program, so that you can refer to it later on.

 ## Printing from the Web

You can print out any Web page that is displayed in your browser window. To do this, make sure your printer is turned on, then open your browser's *File* menu and click on *Print....*

A Print dialog box will appear. You can find out how to complete this on page 20. When you have finished, click on the OK button. Your computer will print out the Web page.

abc abc Copying text

These instructions explain how to copy text from a Web page into a word processing program, such as WordPad.

1 Open your browser and display the Web page.

2 Select the text that you want to copy with your mouse.

3 Open your browser's *Edit* menu and click on *Copy*.

4 Open WordPad. Open the document into which you want to insert the text from the Web page.

5 Position the cursor where you want the text to appear. Open WordPad's *Edit* menu and click on *Paste*.

6 The text from the Web page will appear in the WordPad document. Follow the instructions on page 12 to save the document.

These screen shots show you what you will see as you copy text from a Web page into a word processing program.

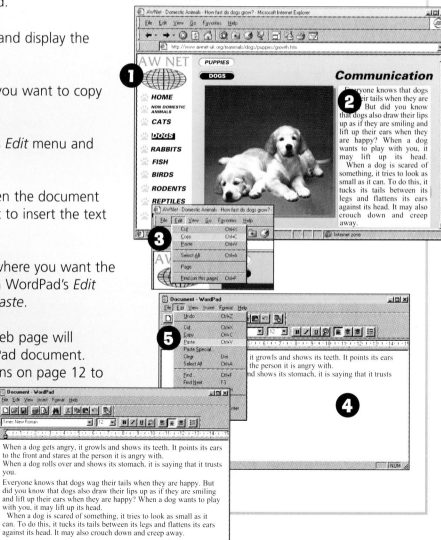

ⓒ How can I use Web information?

The general rules for using information from CD-ROMs (see page 27) also apply to using information from the Web.

Many Web sites include a page of "copyright information". This states what you can and can't do with the information on the site. Always obey the rules and restrictions. If you don't, you may be breaking the law.

❓ Is it accurate?

Unlike a CD-ROM, not all the information on the Web is provided by experts. Anyone can put information on the Web. This means that a lot of it is opinion rather than solid fact, and some of it is inaccurate. Before using any information from the Web, try to double-check it against other sources, such as a book or a CD-ROM.

★ Copying pictures

These instructions explain how to copy a picture from a Web page into a painting program, such as Paint, or a word processing program, such as WordPad.

❶ Open your browser and display the Web page.

❷ Position your mouse pointer over the picture, then click on the right mouse button.

❸ A menu will appear. Click on *Copy*.

❹ Open WordPad, then open the document into which you want to insert the picture. Position the cursor where you want the picture to appear. Alternatively, open Paint.

❺ In WordPad or Paint, open the *Edit* menu and click on *Paste*. The picture will appear in the WordPad or Paint document. Follow the instructions on page 12 to save the document.

These screen shots show you what you will see as you copy a picture from the Web and paste it into a word processed document.

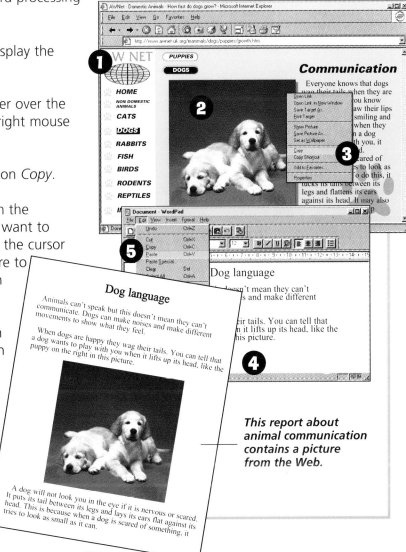

This report about animal communication contains a picture from the Web.

Ça va?

Ça va bien, merci.

Languages on-line

A good way to improve your skills in a foreign language is by reading and listening to information in that language. There are many sites in other languages on the Web. You will also find useful reference tools such as language dictionaries.

Dictionaries on the web

If you come across a word you don't know when you are doing your foreign language homework, you could use an on-line language dictionary to look up its meaning in English.

You will find many different dictionaries at Travlang's Translating Dictionaries site. It's at **http://dictionaries.travlang.com**/. The home page contains hyperlinks to all the dictionaries on the site. Click on the hyperlink to the one you require. For example, to see a dictionary that translates German words into English, you would click on <u>German -> English Dictionary</u>.

A German-English dictionary on the Web

Type a word here, then click on Submit.

The translation of the word appears here.

Sites in other languages

Some Web sites in other languages, including the ones on the right, are aimed specifically at people who are learning that language. The text is simplified and may be accompanied by a translation. They often include interesting facts about countries where the language is spoken.

To find a site in the language you are learning, try using a search engine. For key words, you could combine the name of the language you are learning, for example, **Italian**, with one or more of these words: **beginners**, **learn**, **lesson**.

These pictures show a selection of Web sites for language learners.

http://www.zipzapfrance.com/

http://www.englishtown.com/

http://www.lingolex.com/spanish.htm

http://www.goethe.de/z/jetzt/eindex.htm

Listen and learn

Some Web sites offer you the opportunity to hear the correct pronunciation of foreign words. (Find out on page 44 what equipment you need to hear sounds on your computer.) The instructions below explain how to use a site called "Foreign Languages for Travelers".

1 Open your browser and type in this URL:
http://www.travlang.com/languages/

2 When the page appears, select the language you speak from the drop-down list.

3 Scroll down the page and click on the hyperlink for the language you are learning, for example, Spanish. Another Web page will appear.

4 Click on a category of words, such as Basic Words or Numbers. Then, click on the Submit button.

5 A list of words and their translations will appear. Click on one to hear how to say it. (Your computer may display a dialog box called File Download. If so, select the option called *Open this file from its current location*, then click on OK.)

A File Download dialog box

6 A small window will appear. After a few seconds your computer will play a recording of the word.

Below are some screen shots from the "Foreign Languages for Travelers" site.

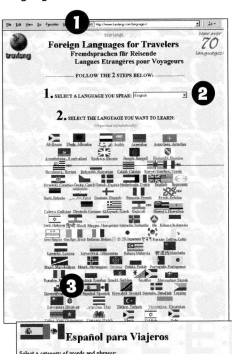

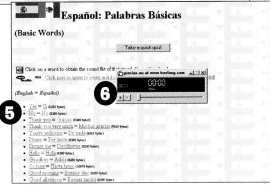

Exchanging messages

You can make learning a new language more exciting by communicating with people who already speak it. E-mail (see page 28) is a good way of communicating with people in other countries, because it is less expensive than international telephone calls and quicker than ordinary mail.

E-mail addresses

With e-mail, as with ordinary mail, you need to know someone's address before you can send them a message. The company that provides you with access to the Internet (see page 43) will give you your own e-mail address.

You can find the addresses of people to correspond with by e-mail on the Web. Some Web sites include lists of young people all over the world who are looking for e-mail correspondents, known as e-pals or keypals.

Look for an e-pal

Follow the instructions below to look for an e-pal on a site called Kids' Space Connection.

1 Open your browser and type in the URL of the Kids' Space Connection PenPal box: **http://www.ks-connection. org/penpal/penpal.html**. You will see several letterboxes. Each one represents an age group.

2 Click on the letterbox for your age group. A list of messages from children looking for e-pals will appear.

3 Read the messages and carefully write down the names and e-mail addresses of anybody to whom you want to send a message.

A sample e-mail address

olivia@cyberspace.com

If you don't find anybody suitable on the Kids' Space Connection Web site, you could leave your own message. You will find instructions for doing this on the Web site. It would be a good idea to mention in your message which language you want to try to improve.

These screen shots are from the Kids' Space Connection Web site.

⚠ Do not give out your address or telephone number when you leave messages on the Web or send e-mail messages to strangers.

E-mail software

To send messages via e-mail, you need to use an e-mail program. There are a number of different programs available, but most of them work in a similar way.

The examples in this book show one called Microsoft Outlook™ Express. It comes free with Microsoft Windows 95 and 98. Find out how to open it on page 45.

Sending and receiving messages

Follow the instructions below to prepare and send an e-mail message.

1 Open your e-mail program. Click on the Compose Message button on the toolbar. A new message window will open.

2 Click on the right of the word "To...", and type the e-mail address of the person to whom you are writing.

3 Click on the right of the word "Subject", then type a brief title for your message.

4 Click in the main part of the window and type your message.

5 To finish, click the Send button. Your message will disappear. It will be stored, ready for sending, in a folder called the Outbox.

6 Click on the Send and Receive button. Your computer will connect to the Internet and send all the messages stored in the Outbox. If there are any new messages for you, your computer will collect them, and put them in a folder called the Inbox.

7 To open the Inbox, click on its icon. You may see a list of titles of messages.

8 To read a message, click on its title.

9 The message will appear in the lower part of the Inbox.

These pictures show you what you will see when you use Microsoft Outlook Express to prepare, send and receive e-mail messages.

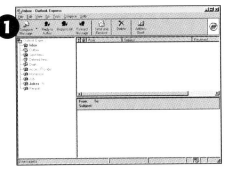

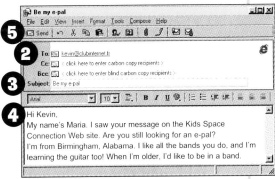

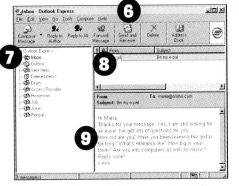

If you are charged by the minute for the time you are on-line, disconnect from the Internet before reading your messages.

Homewor k help

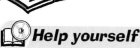

There are several Web sites where you can get help on a range of subjects, from science to art, for free. These sites invite you to send in questions which will be answered by experts such as teachers and university students.

Help yourself

You should always try to do your homework by yourself before you ask other people for help. Try looking for the information you need in a book, on a CD-ROM, or on the Web. Then, if you are really stuck, make a note of specific questions to send in to a "homework help" site.

Finding homework help sites

To find homework help sites like the ones shown below, use a search engine (see page 32) to look for the key phrases **"ask an expert"** or **"homework help"**. Some homework help sites offer to help you with any subject. Others specialize in one subject.

Below is a selection of homework help sites that are available on the Web.

Cyberpapy at http://www.cyberpapy.com/

Mad Scientist Network at http://www.madsci.org/

You will find addresses for other homework help sites on page 42.

Dr. Math at http://forum.swarthmore.edu/dr.math

Using homework help sites

When you go to a Web site that provides help with homework, the first thing you should do is make sure that your question hasn't already been asked and answered. Most homework help sites contain Web pages listing the questions that have already been sent in, with the experts' answers. These pages are often known as the archives.

Look through the archives to see if you can find your question. In some archives, the questions are divided into subject categories. Other archives include a search engine that will locate questions containing key words or phrases for you.

Q Asking questions

When you are sure that nobody else has asked your question, look around the Web site for a way of sending in your question. You will find either an e-mail address to send your message to, or a form to complete. You may have to click on a hyperlink, called something like Send a question or Post a message, to find the e-mail address or form.

Remember to ask the experts specific questions but don't expect them to do your work for you. For example, if you have a list of percentages to calculate, don't submit the whole list of problems. Instead, send in a sample problem and ask the expert to explain how to calculate percentages.

40

A Obtaining an answer

Some homework help sites answer your questions by e-mail (see page 38). These sites ask you to supply your e-mail address when you ask a question. Other sites will put the answer to your question on a Web page. You will have to go back to the Web site later and check to see whether your question has been answered.

The experts will reply as quickly as they can, but don't expect an immediate reply. Homework help sites receive a great number of questions. They rely on volunteer experts to answer the questions in their free time. You may have to wait a day, or even several days, before you receive an answer.

Asking an expert

These instructions explain how to get help with your mathematics homework from a typical homework help Web site.

1 Open your browser and type the URL of a homework help site into the address box. You will find a list of URLs on page 42.

2 Click on the subject you need help with, for example MATH. A Web page containing a search engine will appear.

3 Type a key word for your question, for example **sequences**, in the blank strip, then click on Search.

4 A list of previously asked questions will appear. If you see your question, or a similar one, click on it to read the answer.

5 If you don't see any relevant questions, look around the Web site for a hyperlink which will enable you to send in your question. A form will appear.

6 Complete the form by clicking in the boxes and typing the requested information, such as your name and question. To finish click on Send. An expert will answer your question in an e-mail message.

You will see screen shots similar to these if you use a homework help Web site.

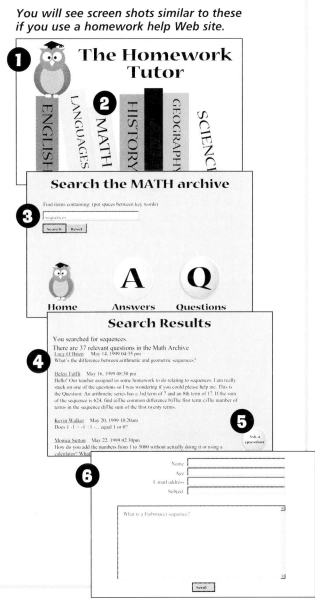

Web sites tour

Here is a selection of Web sites that you might find useful as you research your homework.

 ## Search services

Yahoo!: **http://www.yahoo.com/**
Yahooligans!: **http://www.yahooligans.com/**
Excite: **http://www.excite.com/**
Hotbot: **http://www.hotbot.com/**
Lycos: **http://www.lycos.com/**
WebCrawler: **http://www.webcrawler.com/**

 ## Encyclopedias and dictionaries

Encyclopedia.com: **http://www.encyclopedia.com/**
Knowledge Adventure Encyclopedia: **http://www.letsfindout.com/**
Compton's Encyclopedia Online: **http://www.comptons.com/**
Microsoft Encarta Online: **http://www.encarta.msn.com/**
Webster Dictionary: **http://www.m-w.com/netdict.htm**
Roget's Internet Thesaurus: **http://www.thesaurus.com/**

 ## News and current affairs

CNN: **http://www.cnn.com/**
BBC: **http://news.bbc.co.uk/**
Microsoft Network: **http://www.msn.com/**
Scholastic News Online: **http://www.scholastic.com/scholasticnews/index.htm**
Time for Kids: **http://www.timeforkids.com/**
Tomorrow's Morning: **http://www.morning.com/**
Oneworld: **http://www.oneworld.org/**

 ## Science

The Lab: **http://www.abc.net.au/science/default.htm**
Exploratorium: **http://www.exploratorium.edu/**
Smithsonian Institution: **http://www.si.edu/**
National Air and Space Museum: **http://www.nasm.edu/**
Science 4 Kids: **http://www.kapili.com/research/index.html**
Bradford Robotic Telescope: **http://www.eia.brad.ac.uk/btl**
Science 4 Kids: **http://www.ars.usda.gov/is/kids/**

 ## Homework sites

Answers.com: **http://www.answers.com/**
Homework Help: **http://www.startribune.com/homework/**
Links to experts: **http://www.cln.org/int_expert.html**
More links to experts: **http://njnie.dl.stevens-tech.edu/curriculum/aska.html**
For students in the UK only: **http://www.bbc.co.uk/education/bitesize/askteach.htm**
Schoolwork Ugh!: **http://www.schoolwork.org/**
Kids Web: **http://www.npac.syr.edu/textbook/kidsweb/**

 ## History and geography

National Geographic Online: **http://www.nationalgeographic.com/main.html**
HyperHistory:**http://www.hyperhistory.com/online_n2/History_n2/a.html**
Castles for Kids: **http://www.castlesontheweb.com/search/Castle_Kids/**
Eyewitness: **http://www.ibiscom.com/**
CIA World Fact Book: **http://www.odci.gov/cia/publications/factbook/index.html**
GeoGlobe Interactive Geography: **http://library.advanced.org/10157**
Volcano World: **http://volcano.und.nodak.edu/**
50 States: **http://www.50states.com/**

 ## E-pals

E-pals: **http://www.epals.com/**
Kidlink: **http://www.kidlink.org/**
Cyberkids: **http://www.cyberkids.com/connection/**
Key Pals: **http://www.reedbooks.com.au/heinemann/global/global1.html**
NetPals: **http://www.eduweb.co.uk/**

 ## Art and literature

Just For Kids who Love Books: **http://www.geocities.com/Athens/olympus/1333/kids.htm**
Web Gallery of Art: **http://sunserv.kfki.hu/~arthp/index.html**
Art Mystery: **http://www.eduweb.com/pintura/**
The Children's Literature Web Guide: **http://www.acs.ucalgary.ca/~dkbrown/index.html**

 ## Hot homework sites

If you think that a Web site will be useful another time, you can create a shortcut to its home page. This will enable you to go to the page without typing out its URL.

To create a shortcut to a Web page displayed in Microsoft Internet Explorer, click on *Add to Favorites...* on the *Favorites* menu. A dialog box will appear. Click with your mouse next to the words "No, just add the page to my favorites", then click OK.

To see a list of the shortcuts you have made, click on *Favorites* on the menu bar. To use a shortcut to a Web page, simply click on its name. Your browser will download the page.

Getting connected

On this page you will find out how to connect your home computer to the Internet.

 ## Internet equipment

The usual way to connect your computer to the Internet is with a telephone line. To do this, you need a device called a modem. This enables your computer to exchange information with other computers across telephone lines. You can find out more about modems on page 44.

Once you have a modem, you need to find a company called an Internet Service Provider (ISP) which will enable you to connect your computer to the Internet.

 ## An ISP

An Internet Service Provider is a company that owns some computers that are permanently connected to the Internet. These computers are like doorways to the Net. When you connect your computer to one of them, you can use the Web, e-mail and other Internet facilities.

An ISP will advise you exactly what computer equipment you require to use Internet facilities. They will supply the software you need, and will provide help by telephone with installing it and connecting to the Internet. They will also give you an e-mail address.

Most ISPs charge for their services, usually every month. A few companies provide Internet access for free.

 ## What costs can I expect?

Some Internet Service Providers charge customers according to the amount of time they spend on-line. Others charge the same amount each month. Some companies also ask for a one-off payment, called a start-up fee, when you start using their services.

Companies that provide Internet access for free may charge customers for certain services. For example, you may have to pay to use the telephone helpline. Also, they may not offer all the services that other ISPs do.

You may have to pay your telephone company each time you go on-line. If you do, make sure that this will only cost the same as making a local telephone call.

 ## Finding an ISP

You can find the names, addresses and telephone numbers of Internet Service Providers in your area in computer magazines and telephone directories.

To choose an Internet Service Provider, telephone a few companies and ask them exactly what services they provide, and how much they charge. It's a good idea to ask friends who are already on-line for recommendations.

 ## The Internet away from home

You can try out the Internet in other places than your home. You may be able to use it at school or in a library. Some places that sell books or computers have computers on which you can explore the Net. Alternatively, you could go to a "cybercafé". This is a type of café where you can pay a small fee to use computers that are connected to the Net.

This girl is using the Net in a cybercafé.

Essential equipment

To follow all the instructions in this book, you need a computer that includes the equipment described below. If your computer doesn't have all this equipment, you will still be able to use it for some pieces of homework. Alternatively, you could add extra equipment to it.

A printer

You will need a printer to print your work onto paper. If you don't have a printer of your own, you may be able to use a printer at school or at a friend's house.

To move your work onto another computer, you will need to use a portable storage device, such as a floppy disk. To save your work onto a floppy disk, follow the instructions on page 12. At step 4, put a floppy disk into your computer's floppy disk drive. This is a slot in your computer's system unit (the box with the on/off button). Click on the icon called 3½ Floppy (A:), then continue from step 7.

A CD-ROM drive

To display the information on CD-ROMs (see page 22), your computer needs a CD-ROM drive. You usually open and close a CD-ROM drive by pushing a button on your computer's system unit. An open CD-ROM drive looks like a tray with a circular hollow in it.

CD-ROM speed

CD-ROM drives work at different speeds, such as 8 speed (8x) and 16 speed (16x). It may say on the front of CD-ROM drive what speed it works at. If not, look in your computer's manual. Before you buy a CD-ROM, make sure it will work on the kind of CD-ROM drive your computer has.

Sound equipment

To play sounds on a multimedia CD-ROM and on the World Wide Web, your computer needs a device called a sound card. This fits inside your computer's system unit. You will need to attach speakers or headphones to your computer so that you can hear the sounds it is making.

A modem

A modem is a device which enables your computer to exchange information with other computers across a telephone line. You will need a modem to connect your computer to the Internet.

There are two main types of modems: internal and external. An internal modem fits inside your computer. Most new computers are sold with internal modems. An external modem sits on your desktop and is connected to your computer by a cable. Both internal and external modems have cables which plug into a telephone socket.

Modem speed

Modems transfer information at different speeds. Modem speed is measured in bps (bits per second). If you decide to add a modem to your computer, choose the fastest one you can afford. Ideally, it should transfer information at no less than 28,800 bps. The faster your modem works, the less time you will spend transferring information from the Internet onto your computer. It is particularly important to have a fast modem if you pay according to the amount of time you spend using the Internet.

Starting computer programs

There are two main ways of starting computer programs with Microsoft Windows 95 and 98. For Internet Explorer and Outlook Express, you will find it quicker to use the first method. For WordPad, Paint, Windows Explorer and CD-ROMs, you will need to use the second method.

Your computer's desktop

To start computer programs, you need to know your way around a part of your computer called the desktop. This is the display that you see on screen when your computer has finished starting up. It will look something like the one shown below.

A desktop

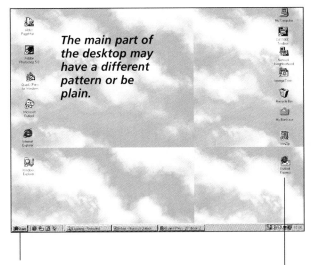

The main part of the desktop may have a different pattern or be plain.

This button is called the Start button.

These small pictures represent different programs or parts of your computer.

Method 2

You can open any program on your computer by choosing its name from a menu. To do this, click with your mouse on the Start button. A list called the Start menu will appear. Rest your mouse over the item called *Programs.* Another list called the Programs menu will appear. Many of the programs on your computer will be listed here. To start Windows Explorer, click on the item called *Windows Explorer.*

To open WordPad or Paint, rest your mouse over the word *Accessories* on the Programs menu. Another menu called the Accessories menu will appear. Finally, click on either *WordPad* or *Paint* on the Accessories menu to start that program.

This picture shows some Windows menus.

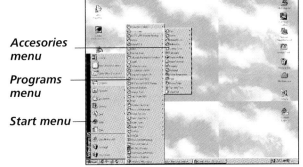

Accesories menu

Programs menu

Start menu

Method 1

Windows 95 and 98 include shortcuts for starting some programs, including Internet Explorer and Outlook Express. These shortcuts appear as small pictures, known as icons, on the desktop. To start a program, simply double-click on its icon.

To start Internet Explorer, click on this icon.

Starting CD-ROMs

To start a multimedia CD-ROM which you have put into the CD-ROM drive, open the Programs menu and look for the name of the CD-ROM or the company that made it. For example, for the *Microsoft® Encarta Encyclopedia*, you will see *Microsoft Reference.* Rest your mouse over this item. Another menu will appear. Click on the name of the CD-ROM, for example, *Encarta Encyclopedia* and the CD-ROM will start.

Using your keyboard

This section explains how to use your keyboard to type words and numbers into computer programs. You will also learn how to correct any mistakes you make as you type.

 A keyboard

Letters, numbers, punctuation marks and other symbols are known as characters. Most of the keys on a keyboard are for typing characters.

They are called character keys. The other keys on a keyboard are known as control keys. You can find out what some of them do below.

This picture shows you where you will find important control keys on a keyboard.

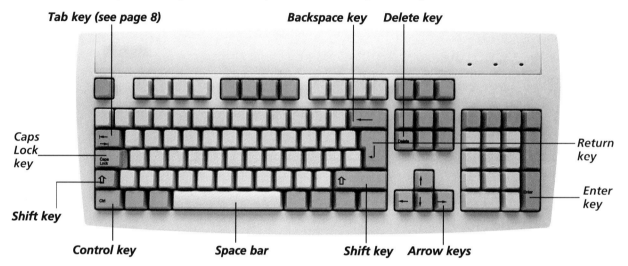

Tab key (see page 8) — Backspace key — Delete key — Return key — Enter key — Caps Lock key — Shift key — Control key — Space bar — Shift key — Arrow keys

 As you type

In a word processing program like WordPad, the cursor moves as you type. It flashes on the right of the character you typed last to indicate where the next character you type will appear.

Each time you reach the end of a line, your computer automatically places the next word you type on the following line.

 Correcting mistakes

You can easily remove any characters or spaces that you type by mistake. Press the Delete key to remove the character to the right of the cursor. Press the Backspace key to remove the character to the left of the cursor. To remove more than one character, press the appropriate key as many times as necessary.

 Moving around

You can move the cursor around the part of the page that already contains text. This enables you to add or change letters in words you typed earlier. It is useful when you make a spelling or typing mistake, and when you forget to include a particular piece of information in your work.

One way of moving the cursor is by pressing the arrow keys. To move it quickly up or down several lines, keep the appropriate arrow key pressed down. You can also move the cursor with your mouse. As you move the pointer over the area of the page that already contains text, it changes into an I-shaped symbol like the one shown here. Place the pointer where you want the cursor to go, then click with your left mouse button. The cursor will jump to the place where you clicked.

A Typing

These instructions explain how to type different types of characters and spaces.

1 To type a letter, press the key which has that letter on it.

2 To type a capital (upper case) letter, hold down the Shift key and press the letter key you want. Then, release the Shift key.

3 To leave a space between two words, press the Space bar.

4 To start a new line before you come to the end of the previous one, press the Return key.

5 To miss a line, press the Return key twice.

6 When a key has two characters on it, press the key to type the bottom character. To type the top one, hold down the Shift key as you press the character key.

7 To type several capital letters in a row, press the Caps Lock key. Then type the letters. When you have finished, press the Caps Lock key again.

This shows what you will achieve by following the instructions above.

7

FORMS OF ENERGY

2 Energy can exist in many forms and the different forms make different things happen. As well as heat, light and sound, there are other forms such as chemical energy, kinetic energy and potential energy.

4 Chemical energy is energy that is released during chemical reactions. Food and fuels, such as coal, oil, and petrol, as well as batteries, are stores of chemical energy.

A Typing skills

If you aren't used to typing, you may find it takes a long time to locate the keys on the keyboard. With practice, you will soon get used to where they are and will be able to find them more quickly.

You may want to buy a computer program, known as typing tutor, that can teach you how to type using all your fingers and without looking at your hands. Some typing tutors combine typing lessons with games.

In this game from a program called Mavis Beacon Teaches Typing® , you have to type words quickly and accurately to prevent the penguin from falling in the water.

Index

 Acknowledgements

Every effort has been made to trace the copyright holders of the material in this book. If any rights have been omitted, the publishers offer their sincere apologies and will rectify this in any future edition.

Usborne Publishing Ltd. has taken every care to ensure that the instructions contained in this book are accurate and suitable for their intended purpose. However, they are not responsible for the content of, and do not sponsor, any Web site not owned by them, including those listed below, nor are they responsible for any exposure to offensive or inaccurate material which may appear on the Web.

Photographs
Cover Rocket courtesy of NASA; Einstein: Hulton Getty.
Computer courtesy of Hewlett-Packard.
p3 International Space Station courtesy of NASA.
p28 Mars courtesy of JPL/NASA/Caltech.
p43 Cybercafé: Image copyright 1999 PhotoDisc, Inc.
p46 Keyboard by Howard Allman.

Software screens
Microsoft® Windows 95 and 98, Microsoft® Encarta® 98, Microsoft® Internet Explorer and Microsoft Outlook™ Express are either registered trademarks or trademarks of Microsoft Corporation in the United States and/or other countries.
Screen shots and icons reprinted by permission from Microsoft Corporation.
p3 "Le Louvre, collections & palace" CD-ROM: coproduced and coedited by Montparnasse Multimedia and la Réunion des Musées Nationaux. ©Montparnasse Multimedia and la Réunion des Musées Nationaux, 1997. All rights reserved; Louvre Pyramid: Architect I.M. Pei ©E.P.G.L. Photo ©RMN/G.Blot.
p22 BodyWorks 5.0 ©1999 The Learning Company, Inc.
p22-24 The Usborne Animated Children's Encyclopedia.
©1998 Usborne Publishing and Great Bear Technology.
All rights reserved.
p47 Penguin Crossing from "Mavis Beacon Teaches Typing® v.8."- the number one typing software.

Web sites
Cover Homework Help. ©1999 Star Tribune.
p3 www.letsfindout.com/, courtesy of Knowledge Adventure, Inc ©1999 Knowledge Adventure, Inc. All rights reserved. Knowledge Adventure is a registered trademark of Knowledge Adventure, Inc.
p28 Mars Surveyor. ©1998-99 California Institute of Technology. All rights reserved. Further reproduction is prohibited; EL PAÍS courtesy of EL PAÍS Digital. www.elpais.es/; The Hunterian Museum. ©Hunterian Museum and Art Gallery, University of Glasgow. Reproduced with permission.
p32 AltaVista images courtesy of The AltaVista Company; Lift Off to Space Exploration courtesy of NASA's Marshall Space Flight Center; Alex Michael Bonnici's space exploration page courtesy of Alex Michael Bonnici; Smithsonian Institution Web pages courtesy of the Smithsonian Institution.
p36 travlang's Translating Dictionaries and Foreign Languages for Travelers. ©1995-1999 travlang; ZipZapFrance: created by Geneviève Brame and the Cultural Department of the French Embassy in London; Englishtown: ©English First, B.V. Learn Spanish used with permission; Jetzt Online: GOETHE INSTITUT MÜNCHEN e.V.
p38 Kids' Space Connection courtesy of Kids' Space.
p40 Cyberpapy, the site which links seniors with juniors to help them with their school homework. Used with permission; Mad Scientist Network courtesy of Washington University; Dr. Math is developed by The Math Forum, Swarthmore College, with funding from the National Science Foundation.

First published in 1999 by Usborne Publishing Ltd, Usborne House, 83-85 Saffron Hill, London, EC1N 8RT, England.
www.usborne.com Copyright ©1999 Usborne Publishing Ltd. The name Usborne and the device ∇ are Trade Marks of Usborne Publishing Ltd. *All rights reserved*. No part of this publication may be reproduced, stored in a retrieval system or transmitted in any form or by any means, electronic, mechanical, photocopying, recording or otherwise, without the prior permission of the publisher. UE.
First published in America in 2000.
Printed in Spain.